SYLVIA AND MARSHA START A REVOLUTION!

The Story of the Trans Women of Color Who Made LGBTQ+ History

JOY MICHAEL ELLISON AND TESHIKA SILVER
ILLUSTRATED BY TESHIKA SILVER

Jessica Kingsley Publishers
London and Philadelphia

Sylvia Rivera and Marsha P. Johnson weren't just friends, they were as close as sisters. Strolling arm in arm down Christopher Street, they looked magnificent.

"Sylvia," Marsha cried, "see that girl over there? She looks hungry. Give her a dollar."

"Marsha," said Sylvia, "that's all our money. How will we eat?"

Marsha smiled. "Us? We'll be fine, honey."

"It's not right for these kids to be sleeping on the street," said Sylvia. She remembered what her grandma said when Sylvia wore a dress for the first time. Sylvia had finally felt free, but Grandma frowned. "You're a boy," she said. "Act like it." Sylvia knew she could only act like herself.

Sylvia, like Marsha, was a transgender girl. People thought she was a boy, but she knew differently. She hated seeing other transgender girls suffer just for being themselves, too.

"We've got to do something for girls like us," she told Marsha.

"That's a man in a dress," a woman shouted, pointing.

"Look at me!" Marsha said, twirling. "I'm not a man.
I'm a woman and I always have been."

Sylvia laughed.

Marsha heard a call:

HERE COMES ALICE IN THE BLUE DRESS!

"Oh no," thought Marsha, "that means the cops are coming."
Police could arrest transgender girls for wearing dresses.
She grabbed Sylvia's hand and they ran.

Sylvia panted, "You okay?"

"Honey, I'm tired of being treated so bad," said Marsha.

Sylvia sighed. "Someday girls like us will be able to wear whatever we want. People will call us by the names we choose. They'll respect that we are women. The cops will leave us alone and no one will go hungry."

Sylvia and Marsha talked and talked about making life better for themselves and their sisters. Then on June 28, 1969, they took action.

Sylvia burst into the Stonewall Inn. "Happy birthday, Marsha!"

"Thanks, honey," Marsha said.

They grooved on the dance floor, until Marsha heard a voice yell:

HERE COMES ALICE IN THE BLUE DRESS!

"Oh, no," she thought, "the police."

"That's a man in a dress," a policeman sneered at Marsha.
"Show me your ID or I'll arrest you."

"Not on my birthday," said Marsha.

The police ordered everyone into the street and began making arrests.

"Come on," Marsha yelled.

The two friends rushed toward the police van.

They pushed past the officers, broke open the van door, dragged out their friends, and set them free.

"The revolution!" shouted Sylvia. "It's beautiful."

The next day, everyone on Christopher Street was talking about the Stonewall Rebellion. Sylvia and Marsha strode with pride, like two lionesses, until they heard the call...

HERE COMES ALICE IN THE BLUE DRESS!

"Look at these children with no homes, running from the cops." Sylvia shook her head. "We still got to do something for them."

Marsha frowned. "We're just two friends, trying to survive ourselves."

"We'll give them what we got," said Sylvia. "Friendship. Let's get a house and open it up to all the young sisters living on the streets."

Young transgender girls came from miles around to live with Sylvia and Marsha. Together, they took care of each other. They ate together, laughed together, and struggled together. They became family.

Sylvia and Marsha spent their lives fighting for the survival and rights of transgender people. Through it all, they were best friends. Their memory shines like a star, showing us that with our friends, we can change the world.

FOR KIDS

You can be like Sylvia and Marsha by sharing what you have and by demanding justice for everyone. You and your friends can start a revolution, too!

Learn more about Sylvia and Marsha

Marsha "Pay It No Mind" Johnson was born on August 24, 1945. She was a Black transgender woman. Even though Marsha had very little, she always gave her money and food away to other transgender people who needed help. She loved to make crowns out of flowers. She wrote poems and sang in a group called The Hot Peaches.

Sylvia Rivera was born on July 2, 1951. She was a Puerto Rican-American transgender woman. When Sylvia was 11 years old, she became homeless. She met Marsha in 1963 on Halloween night. Marsha fed her and kept her safe. Together, they dreamed of doing something to make their lives better and change the world for other transgender people. They started a group called Street Transvestite Action Revolutionaries, known as STAR, to help other transgender girls like them.

Sylvia and Marsha were kind, generous, smart, and very brave. They weren't afraid to be themselves and they weren't afraid to tell the truth, even when it made their own friends angry. That made some people afraid of them, but Sylvia and Marsha always stuck together and supported each other.

What does "transgender" mean?

When a person is born, the doctor looks at their body and assigns them a gender. "It's a boy," says the doctor, or "It's a girl!" Gender, however, is about much more than your body. It's what's in your heart and your head that really makes you who you are.

When a person's gender is different from the gender the doctor gave them at birth, that person is transgender. Sylvia and Marsha were transgender women. They lived as women and wore clothes that made them feel good.

There are many different types of transgender people. Here are some common definitions for words about gender:

Transgender	A person whose gender is different from the gender they were assigned at birth.
Transgender girl	A person who the doctor thought was a boy, but who is really a girl.
Transgender boy	A person who the doctor thought was a girl, but who is really a boy.
Intersex	A person whose body isn't easily defined as "male" or "female" due to biological differences on the outside or inside of their body. They can be any gender, just like everyone else.
Non-binary person	Someone who is not a boy or a girl. Their gender might be a mixture of both or something completely different.
Gender fluid	Someone whose gender changes. Sometimes their gender is more like a girl, or a boy, or non-binary. At other times, they might be a different gender.
Agender	Someone who does not identify as being any gender.

What was life like for transgender people when Sylvia and Marsha were young?

When Sylvia and Marsha were growing up, it was very hard to be transgender. Sometimes families did not accept transgender children. Many transgender teenagers became homeless. Few people would give jobs to transgender people, so many transgender people were very poor.

Police often arrested transgender people. In New York and many other places, there were laws that made it illegal for transgender people to dress as they chose. For transgender women of color, like Sylvia and Marsha, life was very dangerous. Police bothered them because they were transgender and because they were people of color and poor. That's why Sylvia and Marsha worked so hard to help other transgender girls, especially homeless transgender girls of color, just like them.

The Stonewall Rebellion

The Stonewall Rebellion was one of the most important events in lesbian, gay, bisexual, transgender history in the United States.

The Stonewall Inn was one of the only places where gay, lesbian, bisexual, and transgender people could be together. Inside the Stonewall Inn, they could dance and have fun, but it still wasn't always safe. Police sometimes came into the Stonewall Inn and arrested people for wearing clothes they thought were wrong. During the Stonewall Rebellion, gay, lesbian, and transgender people said "No" to the police.

There are many different stories of what happened the night of the Stonewall Rebellion. *Sylvia and Marsha Start a Revolution* is a retelling of one version of the events.

Although her birthday was not until August, many people say that Marsha held her birthday party at the Stonewall Inn the night of the Rebellion. When a police officer demanded that Marsha show him her identification, she refused, saying, "I got my civil rights." Sylvia arrived late to Marsha's party and found a huge protest in front of the Stonewall Inn. Transgender girls, homeless gay youth, and other queer people joined together to fight for their rights.

Sylvia and Marsha and everyone else who participated in the Stonewall Rebellion changed the United States forever. Gay, lesbian, bisexual, and transgender people felt proud to be themselves and joined in the fight for their rights. The next year, people in cities across the United States remembered the Stonewall Rebellion by marching and protesting. Today, we still remember the Stonewall Rebellion by having Pride parades.

Can you find these friends of Sylvia and Marsha in *Sylvia and Marsha Start a Revolution*?

Some people say that Marsha was the first to protest during the Stonewall Rebellion. We know for certain she was not alone. You can find in this book pictures of **Stormé DeLarverie** and **Miss Major Griffin-Gracy**, two other Black women who were also at the Stonewall Rebellion.

After the Stonewall Rebellion

After the Stonewall Rebellion, Sylvia and Marsha started a group called STAR, which helped transgender homeless girls. Sylvia, Marsha, and the other girls of STAR lived together. They shared food and helped each other stay safe and happy. They protested for rights and freedom for their transgender sisters.

On July 6, 1992, Marsha died. So many of her friends came to her funeral that it turned into a huge parade in her honor.

Sylvia was heartbroken when her best friend died. For a while, she was sad and alone, but she found a new community. She fell in love with a transgender woman named Julia Murray. She started feeding homeless people again.

Like Marsha, Sylvia fought for transgender people until she died. Sylvia became sick with liver cancer. While she was in the hospital, she asked gay and lesbian leaders to remember that transgender people needed legal rights. She died on February 19, 2002.

Today, people all around the world remember Sylvia and Marsha as friends and leaders.

FOR PARENTS AND TEACHERS

Questions to discuss with your child

- Sylvia and Marsha wanted to make the world better. What kind of a world do you want to live in?

- Sylvia and Marsha always helped their friends. They also made new friends, especially with people who needed help. How can you and your friends help others?

- Sylvia and Marsha knew what their genders were, even though they were different from what other people expected. What gender do you feel like? What kind of clothes do you want to wear?

Resources for learning more about Sylvia and Marsha and other transgender people

You don't have to be an expert to talk about gender with your children. The most important thing you can tell your child is that you love and accept them whatever their gender is. When your child knows they are safe with you, they can feel safe in the rest of the world.

Online resources

- **Queer Kids Stuff:** http://queerkidstuff.com

- **The Family Equality Council:** https://www.familyequality.org

Other books about gender and sexuality

- *It Feels Good to Be Yourself: A Book About Gender Identity* by Theresa Thorn, illustrations by Noah Grigni

- *Julián Is a Mermaid* by Jessica Love

- *47,000 Beads* by Koja and Angel Adeyoha, illustrations by Holly McGillis

- *The Boy and the Bindi* by Vivek Shraya, illustrations by Rajni Perera

- *Love, Z* by Jessie Sima

- *This Day in June* by Gayle E. Pitman, illustrations by Kristyna Litten

- *When Aidan Became a Brother* by Kyle Lukoff, illustrations by Kaylani Juanita

Activities

Make a protest sign!

When transgender people needed help, Sylvia and Marsha held protests. They made signs that told people what they wanted the world to be like. You can do the same.

Materials:

- Cardboard, poster board, or paper

- Markers, crayons, or paint

Step one: Gather your materials. Make sure your sign is the size you like.

Step two: Decide with your child what your sign should say. How do you want the world to be better?

Step three: Write the words on the sign. You can do that for your child, or they can do it themselves.

Step four: Decorate your sign.

When you're finished, you can hang your sign in the window or take it to a protest!

Make a crown like Marsha!

Marsha loved to make crowns out of flowers and other things that she found. Here's how to make one yourself.

Materials:

- Tissue paper of different colors
- Pipe cleaners
- Scissors

Step one: Stack three or four sheets of tissue paper together. With the shorter side of the tissue paper rectangle facing you, make one-inch-wide accordion folds. Flip the stack back and forth until you have folded all of it into a strip. Cut the strip in half.

Step two: Wrap the end of the pipe cleaner around the middle of each strip. Twist the end of the pipe cleaner so it is secure.

Step three: Cut a rounded shape at the end of each strip. This will be the petal of the flower.

Step four: Carefully open the accordion folds on one half of the strip. Pull the top layer away from the rest. Do the same on the other side. Continue separating the layers until your flower blooms.

Step five: Wrap or braid more pipe cleaners around the ends of the pipe cleaner until you form a circle big enough to sit on your child's head. Join the ends of the circle together. You can add more flowers or other objects to the crown, as you like.

Help your community

Sylvia and Marsha Start a Revolution is a great way to encourage children to undertake projects that help other people in their community. Children can practice being like Sylvia and Marsha by raising money, collecting donations, or volunteering. Encourage them to build relationships with the people they help, so the entire community can help each other. Children can spread Sylvia and Marsha's message by inviting their friends to join them.

of related interest

Who Are You?
The Kid's Guide to Gender Identity
Brook Pessin-Whedbee
Illustrated by Naomi Bardoff
ISBN 978 1 78592 728 7
eISBN 978 1 78450 580 6

You Be You!
The Kid's Guide to Gender, Sexuality, and Family
Jonathan Branfman
Illustrated by Julie Benbassat
ISBN 978 1 78775 010 4
eISBN 978 1 78775 011 1

Are You a Boy or Are You a Girl?
Sarah Savage and Fox Fisher
Illustrated by Fox Fisher
ISBN 978 1 78592 267 1
eISBN 978 1 78450 556 1

My Dad Thinks I'm a Boy?!
A Trans Positive Children's Book
Sophie Labelle
ISBN 978 1 78775 221 4
eISBN 978 1 78775 222 1

First published by the author as a Kickstarter edition in 2019
This edition published in Great Britain in 2021 by Jessica Kingsley Publishers
An Hachette Company

1

Copyright © Joy Ellison and Teshika Silver 2021
Illustrations copyright © Teshika Silver 2021

Front cover image source: Teshika Silver.

A CIP catalogue record for this title is available from the British Library and the Library of Congress

ISBN 978 1 78775 530 7
eISBN 978 1 78775 531 4

Printed and bound in China by Leo Paper Products Ltd.

Jessica Kingsley Publishers' policy is to use papers that are natural, renewable, and recyclable products
and made from wood grown in sustainable forests. The logging and manufacturing processes are
expected to conform to the environmental regulations of the country of origin.

Jessica Kingsley Publishers
73 Collier Street
London N1 9BE, UK

www.jkp.com